Other books by
Stewart S. Warren

———————————————

Shape of a Hill

The Weight of Dusk

Second Light

The Song of It:
A Travelogue of Norteño

Essence:
contemplations in image and word
with Corinna Stoeffl

The Sea Always Near

Just One Leaf

Atogaki

solstice edition

Mercury HeartLink

Atogaki

solstice edition

Stewart S. Warren

Atogaki: poems

Solstice Edition: with 28 new and additional poems, December 2010

Copyright ©2010 Stewart S. Warren

ISBN: 9780982730324

Publisher: Mercury HeartLink

Book design by Mercury HeartLink

Front cover photograph by Stewart S. Warren

Back cover portrait photograph by Georgia Santa-Maria

Mercury HeartLink
editor@heartlink.com

Additional copies and other HeartLink publications at: www.heartlink.com

Contents

Introduction

Shattering Grass

The World I Was In

The Sky Here

West of Anywhere

For youth in every country—
for what you know,
for what you must do.

You are never alone.

INTRODUCTION

The Japanese word *Atogaki* refers to an afterward: that piece, for reasons of content, continuity or voice, that doesn't fit into the general flow of a book or body of work, and is inserted at the end. As with American literature, it can be used to talk about how the work came into being or was developed, or to provide further illumination about the process behind the presentation. In Japan, *Atogaki* can also be that device where the author challenges their own work, offers counter arguments to the ideas they have set forth: *"Here are some reasons why the things I've just said are not completely sound."*

Does this collection of poems contradict my other works? Well, not exactly. Not any more than how every idea challenges the one before it, conquering what preceded it to become what's needed next. Yesterday I gave my life to Christ, today the myths belonging to avatars distract me from knowing myself. Both are valid. Life is ambiguity and paradox, the result of investigation and living with your shirt open to the wind. I have been taught to revere conviction and single-mindedness, but honestly, I am wary of them.

The contradictions of my life show up everywhere in my writing. My poems are flakes of mica drifting as dust in a room that is too big to see, illuminated by circumstance and authority beyond their knowing. They're right, right where they are, and always wrong in and of themselves. Poems are flawed. Nevertheless, we need them. Without art, how would we know whether to touch our head or our heart when we pray?

And here I apologize. My loose fact-checking, particularly in earlier collections, places too many stumbling stones on a path already littered with obscurities, tangents, and the machinations of a mind shaped by childhood trauma, LSD and, until my early thirties, way too much alcohol. But that's no excuse. I have invited you to my world, and you have come., I could, however, have baked those cookies a bit longer before setting them on the table.

At times I have spoken as a person who knows things, things about how the world works. At those moments perhaps I did, though I've relied too heavily on that voice, and later questioned my own knowing. But more often, when I go back to those poems I am reminded and comforted by words that, sincerely, I find hard to claim as my own. I, too, am sifting through this stuff, sorting arrogance from truth. When the magic works, I'm as blown away as anyone.

All too often, I choose struggle over peace. I live at the edge of what some call a troubled mind. Calling myself an artist has been an attempt to give some purpose to that (or justification), but I'm not sure I absolutely believe it. Lately I've thought, If I'd have just gone to school and become an engineer, or if I'd have led a simple life of crime, I might not have been so self absorbed and at the same time so concerned with human nature and evolution. Or if I was a farmer growing carrots and rice, I could offer people something to eat, something they really need.

Once I thought: I'll be a looking glass. I will offer the experience of my life as a window through which others will see more clearly into the phenomenon which is their true self. Do you know how a child's kaleidoscope is constructed?

To make this intriguing toy, three strips of mirror are connected on their long sides to form a triangle, which is then fixed inside a tube. At one end of the tube there is a chamber filled (loosely) with colored rocks, at the other an opening through which the eye catches light entering from the opposite end. When rotated in the hands colored stones and other glittery bits are transformed into a fractal world of phantasmagoria. I'd have to say that a kaleidoscope is more of what I've constructed than a looking glass. The poet as magician.

As it turns out, I've written mostly for myself, and hopefully a handful of friends. And this, of all collections, is a particularly difficult one—difficult to write, diffiicult to read. But at this stage of my life I can think of little else that brings a feeling of quiet purpose and satisfaction more than those moments when I'm writing—both the first flush of original creation with pen and notebook and then those delicious stages of editing on the computer. I enjoy it now even more than performing. For some whacky puritanical reason I was ashamed to admit self indulgence in this area. Now I rely upon it, setting aside plenty of time for my work and the work of others. And there are some wonderful poets out there, if you dig.

In this introduction that is a forward to a book that is an afterward, I caution myself. I know less than ever before, including the value of these poems, and the value of my life. I didn't think I'd still be here. What do I know?

One thing I found out is that publishing books is a good way to hide your work and stay off the radar—and that can be a blessing. I watch others struggle with self promotion, and then, maybe fame. Some people handle it well; most do not. For me, making a book can be like writing a letter to yourself, putting it in an envelope with a stamp on it, and mailing it years later. Or, you don't even have to mail it—just keep writing.

Outcomes and conclusions have become less and less attractive, but exploration of the world through poetry and associations with other artists is a divine dance as you dangle blindfolded on the end of plank, a sunrise or sunset always in progress. By the time art has become objects, the sacred juice may have moved on. So, as much as possible, enjoy the process of your own work!

Stewart S. Warren, Albuquerque - 2010

Shattering Grass

MEETING AGAIN
with thanks to William Stafford

And just now I understand
that my muse means
my own way of looking at things.
For reasons we've discussed
that had seemed difficult.
Anyway.
A nearly full moon tonight, tomorrow
Winter Solstice and the eclipse.

Just when you think you'll get the light back,
one last sleight of hand
with black silk and blood candle
    causes the audience
to hold its breath in an O.

Backstage they crank the wheels
of the cosmos, a hand reveals a face,
the light says Ta-Da,
and there, like a moon, your old friend.

BEYOND THE SURFACE

I can feel it there
like a creek bed in my mind,
at the beginning of my body,
where the world comes together
in the wet rock.

Fish dart
then gather in constellations.
    This is the walk I'm on
stepping from stones, ducking
overhanging limbs to take the game trail

quietly on to the green edge—
cattails, sudden honking frogs,
the fish vanished for now
but always turning in heaven
beyond the duty of day.

THE KNOWN ROAD

Because you have been offered
     peace of mind;
because the light of the world
has made invitation and
asked for your help;
because
     you have nothing
and no place to go;

     and because,

as we practiced it
thousands of years ago,
     the shaman
produces a state of death
then brings himself
     back to life
as demonstration

of the true nature of things,
     you already know
the road to your waking.

Evolution Inevitably

Something calls from elsewhere,
a great need or enlistment
like a tide which is the edge of an ocean
where the moon and the spinning
make known
    their working hands.
Night gives way toward a shape
not yet formed, sand shifts and
a thousand mouths run away
under the soles of your feet.

What you thought to hold on to,
a pier or a shelf
or conquests made for movies,
have no way of staying, nor need to.

Learning to listen is sending your head
down a wire, getting out of the way
of what buzzes at the base of your spine.
It seems impossible to get hooked up—
    then, inevitable.

Every time we arrive

at the edge of the known coast
    the call comes through.
Any tower can house the bell that rings.

In the morning you see
a migration of butterflies has settled
in the corn, covered rooftops,
replaced artificial loss
    and other false thoughts
with hands and fins and wings
that cross the sea as one.
You see the wave.

TALKIN' 'BOUT

everybody
wants to
talk about
talk *about me*
shit the music
just make words
rap down
private sound
yakity yak
school kid rhymes
nothin' here
teacher said
use your words
singsong jive
deadpan jaw
numb your gum
stuff your gun
lock yourself
in your room
who cares
others bleed
jaded flowers
sideways shove

talk about
fright as night
blank as day
elect toads
in the head
put the children
in the pen
feed them slop
plug it in
some to war
some to shop
make believe
freedom's end

ABOUT FACE

My Second Life watches itself
through the window, likes
to mouse around.
This is my Fan Page, refuge, identity.
How am I doing?,
    my Second Life asks.
We have rock stars in common.

I'm a gorgeous blonde;
I'm the L.A. Dodgers;
I'm black as the Ace of Streets
all smooth and hard and full of jive.
I'm in a chat room with my enemies;
    I'm checking myself in the mirror.
I have to get up to pee but I
can't break loose.

Away from my laptop
nobody knows me, not the me
all my friends comment on.
I'm often misunderstood.
I change my mood so I change
profile pictures.

It's all about me
and how I vote.
What kind of a puppy are you?

I like Dougie and the Dolphin;
I like Persian Poetry; I like Hug a Tree;
    I like know what's happnin'.
I had to remove your connection
but, baby, I like like your status.

My Second Life is kinda complex;
my Third Life tweets on the side.

WELLNESS
for Lisa

Over breakfast she breaks rules,
tells of the small faraway place
institutions reserve for clients
who want to read their own brain scans.
Making your own money
    and getting help from the system
are two wings of a bird pulled to ripping.

A strong salmon is better
for the ladders she has to go,
    those steep falls
and hook of claws not enough
to block clear pools up ahead.

The problem with getting well
is a case file that keeps
being sent to its room,
off the grid of her ecology.
She looks them in the eye
on her way upstream—
    ocean, mountain,
sunlight in one leaping blink.

SHATTERING GRASS

The twenty one souls of this world
ride the binding current
to nowhere that can be claimed.
Owls gather and lounge like cats, then

at night, which always waits
in the darkness of an unopened drawer,
they lift becoming frost
and fire and silent goodbyes.

Another of the twenty one
is shattering grass—this could be
your clan waving as millions,
what it takes to make a savanna.

Knowing this, you still whistle
under your breath on a dark road
where overreaching trees
come to a dim point

you hope is a friendly house.

THE HANDS OF SIERRA LEONE

*What force or circumstance could cause a people to
cut off the hands of their countrymen—their own
hands—as a way of calling out for help?*

These are my hands, hands axed
and laying in the street, buried
hastily in the bush, dirt floor of my house.

These are my hands palms up, scattered
through the village, calling out
for bodies, for the hands of others.

These are my hands left empty
next to the diamonds they dug for Europe,
plantations that should have been theirs.

These are my hands at the throats
of countrymen and colonials,
my ignored attempts at being heard.

These are my hands cut off at the wrists,
walking on fingers to find the children
rotting in piles, shooing away vultures.

These are my hands at their own funeral,
my lifelong companions, my only means
of feeding myself and my family.

These are my hands hovering
above every deed, watching the wicked,
comforting the frightened and fallen.

These are my hands, thousands of hands,
lifting above the trees, wings waiting
to carry bewildered souls homeward.

These are my hands gathered before you,
waving goodbye to a world that cries
and claws at itself in the dark.

These are the hands of Sierra Leone.

PEACE

This enchantment of Bougainvilleas
may be the last delight, a station
of the cross beyond trial and tribulation.
    On an afternoon gathered
in a corner of the compound where birds
tease at the stillness, sunlight ripples
with gentle shadows over quiet faces.
Any moment—the machine guns.

Any moment the angry young men
correcting nuns, being used
like forks and knives, struggling
with the word "colonial."
Probably our last cup together.

From the tree tops monkeys see us
fighting ourselves;
they scratch their small heads, quick
to turn and run, not always
    quick enough.
A time before wars wants to return,
remember itself as plots of family corn,
a sky without smoke, cities and

babies growing into strong trees
that fall naturally as they pass on their knowing.

In this small courtyard we leave
letters for loved ones, distribute shoes,
shoulder laptops and weapons.
We must go,
but I leave you the peace
of Bougainvilleas, a memory
of something we cannot remember.

FEELING WORDS

There is what I call the
Beginner Set of Feeling Words:
glad, mad, sad, scared.
Sophistication follows.
Anger can be plotted
    on a continuum starting
with miffed, passing through
frustration to pissed and conclusively
murderous rage. All this
nuance of the modern body,
Twenty First Century Psych.
I learned to look inside
for the signs of his coming.

Emotion can be a slippery scale
with changing backdrops,
a deck of expressions, sudden
drop offs, tricky turns, also
a quality in the gut without which
this ship has no keel.
Loss and grief also have weather,

detours, depths—

my cell phone down the toilet,
my dead hamster, my child
in the morgue, entire villages
    deprived of drinking water.
Some storms last
all night. Longer. We feel it.

It wouldn't be night without day,
study without grace.
One of my favorite shapes
    of glad
is pleased satisfaction. It feels
like finding a Chinese box
in the attic, a bar of soft dusty light
making the presentation.
Inside—something small, saved.

Or the satisfaction
of an accomplishment
but not a flag-waving event.
Unexpected bloom of a seven line poem
with hardwood dowels for joints
oiled only with the palms of my hands;
that moment when
    I finally heard you
and it didn't hurt after all;
the suspension of time and duality

on an Autumn day;
a well tossed salad.

Pleased satisfaction arrives
without anticipation, sometimes
    with only a slight effort
to disregard the background voice
of accumulated wrongs—
or maybe no muscle at all,
nothing to oppose, just
    soft mind.

I could say a lot about fear:
the *Uh oh* and *Oh no*
in every minute, a thread
always there to be tugged.
But not now...

this is the light rising or falling
just right, the children's hour,
the old woman with her hands
    in her lap, a Chinese box
that doesn't require opening, a book
of poetry understood,
    or not.

CHANGING HOUSES

Some houses can go backward
and forward, their streets like tunnels
changing mountains and rivers in the dark.

Let's say you start in Poland
hiding a bible in the wall, make it
to the house next door where

you drive a chariot through the kitchen
gathering up the known planets
and dividing things by threes.
If you stay still long enough

you can watch your own childhood
go from house to house looking
for parents, playmates, a coat
that you can wear until it fits.

If you've forgotten something
down at the end of the block
you might have to go back
by way of Korea, a house you set on fire,
    flames that remember your face.

And Immediately I Have Ideas

Phenomenal, he says, the rock
that fell, the one the size of a bus
letting go at that precise
    geo-historic moment, cleaving
a chunk from the dam,

unleashing her power, setting waters free,
causing ravens to caw alarm and fish
to scramble for hidey holes.
Is that really *what happened?*

Engineers will learn to predict
calamities, divert asteroids,
    bend the sun. Seers will say
this is a sign from Nature:
too much intervention, "bad humans."

One way or another I reach in with my mind,
    bring something to it.

I fuss—first with meaning,
then calculation, morals, mechanics.
I forecast. Arrange.

But what is *just seeing?*

Light suspended, void vacuum,
sky crack, mountain dive.
Sound coming like
....nothing, just arriving.

Splinter tree. Tremble feet.
   Water. Concussion. Rumble.
Echo—shift—flash—yell—what.
Can the meaning of this simply
be *presence?*

The Last Word

In my town a man reads books.
The things he reads grow
under his feet and run out
across the land as connecting colors,
colors that go to the tips
of continents, that fan out
in directions of touching, knowing.

Sometimes cities
cross paths in their going,
struggles and great inventions
that play vivid in the making
of mankind. He reads

that an American has conquered
    a waterfall in Uruguay,
bought it for his daughters,
guards its wet mouth ready
to steal last kisses, stands over
the gushing with a sharp knife.
Soon, air may also be private.

He leaves the page and drifts

across prairies, finds civilizations
and other bones half buried
and willing to tell their story.
Long legged birds arrive
    wilted and wondering,
the last water they saw going
down pipes toward dirty oceans.

The history he reads
keeps circling a shrinking streambed.
When does our kind mature?
If we would but let the water fall,
let it advocate for our lives
    the way it knows best,
the way love designed it...

Wondering about the warming,
    then the cooling,
he closes his book and listens
to the redemption of mile-high ice
crawling slow—a sound,
    inevitably,
above all others.

BIG, BIG LOVE

We'll have to do this love
a little at a time:
an orange leaf catching winter light;

migration of whale and pup;
refrain from fear;
gentle reaching within.

The Self seems too big to tackle
all at once, and there are so many
other doors to try.

The door labeled "What if I fail?"
is a popular choice, built
solid as a house.

But if you can see it—
you can see it not.
And so, one house at a time

the world is dismantled,
so-called memory dissolved.
In time these things happen.

In time they were made and so they fall.
In the end, as in the beginning,
"I love you,"

are the only words
worth passing from body to body,
soul to soul.

WE ARE SALT

What has happened down here
hasn't completely happened.
Some will say it was famine,
some will say a fire like the one
in the story, an asteroid, a bomb,
humanity imploding upon itself.

We held one another's hands
as they pushed us into shallow graves.
Sometimes we leapt on our own.
    There's no shame, just
the moment when the world begins
to crack, and there
pulling the trigger and falling into the ground
    is the heart you tried to deny.
The only heart.

What has happened down here
is that we have fallen
    into a stream of star stuff.
Trembling.
We get to know—
but first feel with fumbling fingers—

her warm wet flesh,
the rusty nails and fear of disappearing,
the song of hope welling up
again and again and again.
Of course, you couldn't save us!

Every divorce is complete.
These things have all been written.
A blues piano runs up and down
in the next room, everybody
soothes themselves best they can.
The warriors stand up,
the whores lay down. A child says,
    then I'll be your crook,
push against *me*—find your heart.

What has happened down here
is that we have done what we can.
Walk me to the wedding, the funeral,
the baptism by fire. Hold all the oceans
    with an inward breath,
run your hands along the branches
of the Apricot and Pawpaw,
    along the coastline that cries
with white gulls and memories
of our child's first steps.

What has been destroyed
is no longer needed.
Our grief honors yesterday.
    I sing over your grave
and already the clouds have passed.
No one can hold you accountable
for that last wave. We are salt
and then we are gone.

WEST WITHOUT APOLOGY
letter to the new pioneers

Your town has got to mean more
than a grain elevator,
a taller church, future parking.
On the way in and on the way out
the river teases the rails;
the rails take it all away,
bring it back by way of satellite,
charge extra if you want water and air.
If you're not an authorized vehicle
the pavement has potholes.
    Sidestep politics.
Hawks still hunt here; every moment,
essentially, wilderness.

Even in winter that secret flower
in the folds of the foothills
will keep you
leaning into the wind, coming
forward on tiptoes. Drowsiness
can be call for revolution, sometimes
a good reason to snuggle.

When you tag that train you hope
there's someone at the end of the line,
some poet or code talker
with heart-shaped ears
waiting to receive your testimony.
You might be the snow drifting
through Bridger or Laramie
but where she longs for you
is larger than any longing
you can imagine—
a high bridge on a high street,
high fives beyond the horizon.

Heat vents and percolating waters
down in the Bighorn bubble up
voices of long-gone Shoshone
who warm their thoughts
in lava that remembers the days
before any of us walked.
Now the deer come down nibbling
where steam softens the crust
of protective snow,
    a meal they can eat
while listening to ancestors
whispering deep in the warming.

Across the attempted plain

gray barns lean slack jawed,
antelope (who are actually comedian dogs)
graze, heads down, horns up,
tearing at stubble—this endless circle
of land and skyscape running to the edge.
All the same, us rattlesnakes
have taken to the hills.

At the intersection daughters sing
goodbye to daddies
    sounding so final,
boys roam angry in gangs
or drift up against newly closed doors,
but the bloom that follows this storm
will be fierce in love, take hold
where nothing real has grown.

You may find these memories
useful somewhere along the way:
a rosy cheek unafraid of wind;
streets reborn each morning at four;
    wild Montana dying
in a pool of sunlight in a horse stall;
her voice stern for compassion.

Diversity and expansion always
kept us cracking, tangents

of wanting and restless dreaming.
Now, convergence
will be your savior, harmony
the new word for survival.

Remember us
laying down iron,
driving the first spike, looking west
with you in mind. Remember us
shedding skin in the rocks,
stars piercing like arrows,
    our home and yours
wheeling overhead.

The World I Was In

Orphaned but Not Alone

I've seen the business of this work:
the chain-dragging and blame-shoving,
spinning-eyed zombies standing in line.
    I've seen the origins of war,
and I've seen its end.

He "works the sign"
in front of his bank;
she jumps on the cart, rides it
    around the store.
Someone inserts an idea
and the dream takes a turn:
terrorists, scarcity, difference.
Are you really buyin' this?

A fox in red sprawls across the billboard,
automatic weapon in her arms.
Sex and death—here we go again.
They want her strong and mad—
    easier to control that way.
Now we can double the homicide rate,
sell security with the other hand.

Look what I've done to your fields of corn.
   Look what I've done to your sister,
your money, your water, your air.
I can keep you guessing all day long
which shell the pea is under—
your religion is fear.

Was that you
sitting at the front of the class
wincing at the sight of bullies;
or were you the hell-child in back
coming from behind, waiting
for a chance at righteous rebuttal?

You think it wouldn't be the world
   without cops and robbers,
but take your police work elsewhere.
You can't "straighten up" a crystal.

I've seen the business of this work:
the hot potato of shame
that keeps it all spinning.
And I don't care
   what name you give
to the Voice in Your Blood
or the Signal Behind the Dream.

Either love is—or love is not.

I'm an orphan in this world,
but know, I am not alone.

THE STRANGERS

The tossing and turning knocked
every night, a stranger long gone,
    always returned.
After his divorce dad left the door ajar,
poured the stranger a drink, sat in the dark,
paced the floor, wrestled it to bed.
He held it at bay—best he could.
Later, he died.

Did he owe money to the mob,
or did a plan go wrong during the war—
he came back but his buddy didn't—
or was there a deal, some history
    with an agent of Satan,
something that made him a recluse,
a curse hard to undo?

During the day we went swimming;
he made my lunches with rye and sharp cheese.
We investigated words and science but
the stranger found me anyway. Every night
my mom or my dad had to wake me,
    bring me back, the little lamp

looking behind the chair, around corners.
  My rabbit!

When I was eight a stranger stabbed me in the back.
My parents just watched
while having drinks at the neighbor's.
I felt the blade nearly to my heart.
  I didn't tell anyone about this nightmare.
When you're a child those things really happen,
  and by then I thought maybe
my parents were in cahoots with it.

When I got older it used my voice
to make demonic sounds in my sleep—
almost human a girlfriend said,
the growling of an old man.
I know when the stranger is in town
  so I've learned to sleep alone,
toss and turn on my own.

Now it wants me to own guns and knives;
  it wants me during the day.
I know what my father was afraid of...
The strangers are just little boys
  who live alone
with no one to wake them.

Safe Passage

2:AM is the time
to ride the ferry to Point Bolivar.
13 is the age to be on your own
making the crossing.
The rumbling coming up
through steel plates lets you know
    the torque of engines,
the underworld churning.

Flotation devices, ropes, warnings,
chocks under wheels,
single short blast from the big horn.
I stand forward on the main deck,
learn to step and trust
the boat rising and falling—
the night always out in front,
    behind us, below us.

My cheeks are cool, moist.

Whatever has to do with oil and the navy
guards Galveston Bay, the opening
to a twinkling edgewise mystery.

A cement ship from WW I holds up
a last hand after forty years of going down.
On the seamless horizon, a tanker
disappears. Later, our sister ship
passing portside. *I hear you,*
say the horns to one another.

Passengers on Deck 2, regular people
I imagine, fade into the night
like my parents and my school
who are far from this ocean.
    In the phosphorescence
of fish and swell no hand,
nor harmful word can touch me.
The spray on my face is honest.

We swing wide, make our approach,
reverse engines. Ropes are tossed,
pilings creak and shoulder us in.
    The gulls are asleep now,
no crying in the dark swallowing.
I go ashore, turn, board again.
Back and forth,
    all night,
the destination is safe passage.

Chump Change

Nowadays, some would say
$1.2 million is just chump change.

After my brother's suicide, my dad
asked me if I'd come live with him.
"Buy you a car. Send you to school."
Sticky strings, but not like rules.
I could choose
    to walk around
the sinkhole in the living room,
encourage him to have friends,
ignore his suspicions about the neighbors
who had *listening devices*.

"Gee dad, thanks. But
I think I'll go up to the Ozarks.
I've still got some kickin' around to do."

"Well, this is last time you'll see me, son."
Not much negotiation in that.
I couldn't quit blaming myself for abandoning him.

After all, I was an adult.

I made my choices, *and my bed,*
as his generation would say.

Thirteen years later I mailed a letter
(to his attorney, the only address I was allowed)
and thanked him, sincerely,
    for the things he taught me.
I told him that I loved him.
More importantly,
    I said that I now knew
that he loved me.
Three months after that
his attorney called with brief condolences.
Later, a check for 100 bucks.

I've kept a hole in my pocket
    to prove
it was never the money I wanted,
    hungry or not.
The charities he chose were appropriate:
Presbyterian education for young men,
a reform school for boys—600K each.
If my debt has been to deny myself,
    I'm paid up, ready
for that love I talked about.

Fast Talker

I forget what to say when I'm scared,
    leave out
        important
or let the stories of others pass for true.
I'm slow, I know. I learned
to look out the window when listening
    to drunks, let people
make up the world for me.
Authorities have their own versions.
Not defending myself is a bad habit.

On our return trip from San Francisco
I marveled at the innocence of landscape.
The only thing I brought back
was a Haight Ashbury Times
and that green corduroy coat.
Next week we got busted together
    on the same crime, a pinch
of pot detectives called Sales.

I started my time waiting for trial in County.
Your parents whisked you off
    to the Bahamas. Jeremiah,

you must have been exhausted
after all that questioning.

In a little room barely big enough
for metal table and single chair
the suits leaned over me, said,
Give us ten names, just ten.
I refused—one silence I'm proud of.
    But I wasn't offended,
they asked everybody those questions,
    didn't they?

I turned left toward hard time, snow blowing
through the bars. You walked
down a concourse
    into sunshine.

You were always the articulate one,
clever, so much quicker than the rest.

Jer, sooner or later,
all the sheep come home.

THE WORLD I WAS IN

Because they don't issue sports equipment
in the penitentiary, the purple mark
stamped on his forehead that curved
    like the business end of a hockey stick
was delivered by a pickaxe.
    "You don't have to stand tall,
    but you do have to stand up."
And, No, I don't have to talk tough
to prove this is a gangster poem—
cause it's not.

Out on Gang Number 1 somebody, finally,
had had enough.
I didn't see myself on either end
of that kind of transaction,
but it was the world I was in.
To someone else I looked like a rabbit.

I got there early, seventeen.
But already someone had petted my fur,
caused me to crouch in the corner.
It started when I was still in storybooks,
learning to read drunks and dodge raptors.

Mother said she always wanted boys;
    she said it a little too loud.
I can remember laying next to my father,
fear like a thud, but I can't tell you
what happened—but I would.
They were always at each other's throats.

If you talk soft to a rabbit
with its ears laid back and trembling body
    it will be still—you'll think
it likes to be caressed. Maybe
the bunny starts to think so too.
Later, it dreams the wooden handle
and heft of the iron pick, always confused.
When I start shaking
everything is proof that I'm a sissy
and anybody's rage can become my own,
especially those messages from the womb.
    It's there we share fault.
She feared and hated him!

They had to come in and get me,
    cut me out
while she was drugged.
This is not a gangster poem—
this is the talon of truth
carving its way into flight.

Easy to Trade Places

I thought myself a vampire
with a mortal's heart,
and so I was.
    And when we're though tonight,
so will you be.
Deny your thirst for warm blood,
your quiver at young skin, the sensation
of the hunt; deny it all
and I will reveal your history
stalking
the receding face of earth.

I took my place as the Don
thinking I had come to it alone,
pride and guilt wrapped
in the cloak of each kill, but
it was you who showed me
    the ways of the desert,
the only well in times of drought.
I thought myself a vampire.

Sweet fawn, I know how you long
to stumble, give your life

to an other, even now
your drowsy head falling back,
the thrill of exposing your neck.

Touch the vein there pulsing,
laying gently now in its nest.
Indigo, then crimson—then black.
    See how easy it is to trade places:
a single drop of saliva slipping
from the razor of your cuspid.

Not Receptacle

I am not the man who finally listens
and hears. What you carry
are books on the subject of you,
a morning glory
    with the right conditions
sending out tender tendrils
to the next passerby. I am not
the shrine of your imagination.

I did not abandon you at birth.
Maybe I would have
taped your crayon horse to the refrigerator,
    maybe not—I wasn't there.
I wasn't there when you witnessed the beatings,
and I wasn't there
when you walked home alone,
everything about you different,
secret, stashed under your bed.
Those bullies.

And I am not the one
who is going to save you,
and I am not the one

who didn't save you then.
On this corner there is a curb,
a streetlamp and a vendor.
My roundness is not the next receptacle.

I have listened like the earth
to your falling leaves, held
ceremonies for your burning,
my rake and my broom finally
worn to wooden nothing. Please,
do not mistake this box of matches.

We are all friends here,
    or we could be, but
lover is not another word
for past deeds projected.
I expect kindness, a little
wind before the storm,
a peach with an honest bruise.
I expect the sun to shine.

I'm working on not dodging arrows
before they're shot.
    I'm working the street,
but mostly just feeding the birds.
We're both the next bus to come along.

WHERE THE SALT WAS

One year I went back to my home state,
a place I couldn't name well with words
like prairie, coastal plain, piney woods,
foothills of the Ozarks or just plain windblown,
because after I left there I found plenty of places
where the wind knows everybody's name.

The time I went back stood tall having travelled
alongside me all this while,
but half the houses I lived in
were gone—I mean *gone*
like time couldn't wait
to say none of that happened.
Part of me wanted it that way,
but I guess I wanted to say which ones.

The big houses in town suffered
Hollywood make-overs with asphalt drives;
other places got found by fire and crawling weeds.
What happened to the people
was pretty much like that too.

The houses in my mind—the ones

I always liked— I left where I lived them.
Next day I did a U-turn at Siloam Springs,
braced the wind back across the panhandle,
kissed the sky
turquoise and wide over Tucumcari.

WASHOUT

Was it when I told you that
I'm short on cash, or
when I said that I can't find much
to be passionate about?
    I don't blame you.
We shared the rain in emails—
after the fact or in anticipation.
More than a hawk's distance.

How it fell here is not falling at all.
Everyone shut their windows.
Storm sewers gushed up
paper cups, single untied shoes,
drowned rats with their short coats
    soaked, silky, finally ready
to go anywhere.
I'm doing the best I can
but I don't believe it.

There are no dead birds this morning.
    That surprised me.
Just the usual business of the tree:
leaves and wings and chatter and all;

a mound of laundry by the door,
shirts at the bottom I don't recognize.
    I must find something
to want today, or vacuum.
Is this what you meant by thriving?

THINK OF CLOUD

I don't have a clue, I told her,
making some vague reference
to what I call being in the world.
But really I meant rent, marketing

myself as functional, desirable,
making ends meet;
making it come together
on this side of the river,

this month, this check register.
I mean to say that this is the edge
to which I have pushed myself.
You can't actually see a black hole.

A push-button-voice
at the Museum of Natural Science
persuades, "Think of cloud
as condition." Viola!

The Cumulonimbus condition
of my impending doom arising
from a cell of free floating

anxiety salutes like an anvil.

Building along a frontal lift,
a line of angry indifference
pushes warm moist innocence
up against the wall, heels clicking.

I've been watching videos
of tornadoes. In Texas and Michigan
they've already happened.
What I'm afraid of... has passed.

My storm hangs between
a pauper's loss of freedom
and do-gooders with life support apparatus.
Don't let them lock me up again.

I squeeze the weather I made
tight in my fist, dubious proof of control.
Rain arrives in a gust. Already
a window of light in the west.

Because It Won't Fix

Threats keep arriving, piling up
at a door the paperboy might recognize
as vacation, foreclosure, death.
Some days, when attacks come
as a dark, menacing flock
you think to get a gun,
but then everyone would know
    you're not gone,
you've just been peering through curtains,
holing up like the train robber
you think yourself to be.

You say you'll get to the bottom of this—
an event revealed, a reason,
some victimization or flaw in the code,
any distraction
to keep running from the wickedness
that thinks itself the whole house,
    the mistake you call you.
Any minute now, you'll fix it,
but do you really believe it?

Every so often there's nothing to do but

   sit yourself down
in a kitchen chair and pull splinters
that feel like the hatchets
you learned—like everyone else—
when it was your turn in the barrel.
But "every so often"
hasn't been good enough. One day,
you'll have to quit ripping at skin,
accept even the cutter
   holding the blade.
There's nothing, really, to figure out.

OPPORTUNITY

Years ago, before fractals
showed radio bums how to bend antennae
small enough to fit into cell phones,
we would have walked all the way back,
but not in time to beat the setting sun.

Now, halfway around the frozen lake
everything lay to the west:
thin twinkle of town lights, last geese
going south across the Bitter Roots,
shovels and tow strap in other vehicles.

The drift we'd plowed, but failed to cross,
pulled us with each surge of spinning
deeper into the ditch, valor resigning,
    the low arc of diffused light
bleating through tree silhouettes.

The two hours it took the tow truck
from Bozeman gave the wind time
    to find us, to fold the car
more completely into the white landscape.
Each pair of lights skirting the shore

could be the help we called for.
We commented on shades of silver,
took photos of light on ice,
let dusk cover what went unsaid.

A dark eagle turned again and again
in the pale silence between ranges;
a doe and a buck passed knee deep
through winter's solution;
flakes of sculpted ice tumbled
    with fine snow
across the freezing, beyond the bridge.
We must have thought that nothing more
needed to be said.

STREAK OF FIRE

And one day I was old—
the great relief of it.

I had kept myself young flirting
with girls, and in my teens and twenties
sometimes with boys.
Shelter is shelter and I moved
    in and out, dangling romance
like a jewel passing for celestial wonder,

a shooting star just beyond reach.
I wrote stories across the night
    that disappeared into possibility, back
into the nothing from whence they came.
I made them as brilliant as I could,
collaborated with other designers.
Much holy scattered dust.

You have to work at keeping up:
fashion, culture, spiritual trend,
the talking blues to hip hop,
hand jive, blogging, vampires.
You have to believe

it's going somewhere.
You have to believe in deliverance.
When you're young

belief is a tank of gas, something
that can be pointed.
Running on empty is a hidden blessing.
    A back road on the desert is
a good place to stop. Here or there,
there's nothing wrong with happiness.

I stood in a circle once and watched
a Hopi elder trickle a trail of cornmeal
    into the center, say his peace,
leave a line of dust, like a comet,
on his way out. That night
the wind erased it all.

When we speak of such things
neither of us is old.

Flit-flit Birds

In a tall slot canyon with fluted walls
rosy as ears with the sun
glowing through them, we stopped—
shifting sand, smell of dry desert rock,
    juniper ushering flit-flit birds
from here to other here's.
"Reincarnation may be just another
construct," I said, "complete with emotions,
manufactured memories."
I was sure all those words meant something—
I had said them.

Smiling that knowing-woman-way
(not one to argue the small stuff)
you said, "Then it's genetics
of our ancestors that makes us
    feel familiar. It's for them
we have catching up to do."
Another round of cheeping birds in and out,
sunlight each time we turned
a corner, the air a bit smitten.

The canyon became hills pinching together,

rising into one of innumerable fingers
flowing down from the mountain.
Up on top, a crow—a second one circling.
   I'm done
with falling in love, I thought,
morning wind still gentle, skipping
down to the river then up and up
through layers of diminishing blue.
If I had already recognized you
I wasn't going to say so.

"I was sick for a long time;" you said,
"when it was over every living thing
glowed for months."
On our way down, the wind-sculpted stone
   caused us to turn together,
a trail we could have said we chose.
Already I was planning the things
I would bring, and the things I wouldn't need
the next time we came.
The crows just laughed.

I'll Be Moving Along

I don't have a plan
and I don't have a means.
I'm moving with the sun.
    Sweeteners: yellow, blue, pink.
One of them will kill me, so
I rotate, play roulette, pick my way
across this perfidious field.
    I have no excuse for this,
and any moment I'm going to
slap my silly ass out of this seat.
I'm going to air up the tires and
    tell someone all this matters,
they matter, I matter.

The open road's not what it used to be—
mom and pop truck stops
a thing of the mind. Anymore
    no one even bothers
to remove the price tags
from respect and generosity. Fuck it,

I'm going on down to Hell—I'm expected—
look up some family members there,

kick some butt.
Then, maybe, I'll drift for a while,
split wood, wash dishes, raise the dead,
    find a friendly music commune
tucked back in an edgewise galaxy.
I might even coast over to Heaven,

see what all the fuss is about;
but those kind of places don't hold me long.
I'd rather scratch up a little fire
here by the river, wait for you
to stumble into camp with an appetite
    and that song about the sea
and the girl and the unreasonable wind.

Given Mornings

It takes two minutes
for the sun to set rim to rim,
extinguish itself
in the rising of someone else's morning.
I have said goodbye too many times.
I say it now
    before you say it,
before it's too late.
But I mean to say, hello.

Hello, to the Daffodils and Nandinas
who watched over me,
to the strong chocolate women
who raised me on the side,
to my mother in long cotton skirt
    from which emerged
the round-cornered stove, cherry cobbler,
cool wash rags, Tchaikovsky,
Treasure Island tucked in for bed.
Hello, to those mornings
    before history demanded retribution,
before television brought monsters.

Before the world was "hurry up,
we'll be late," it was
galoshes by the register, naps,
Orange French Toast.
It was okay to spill my milk.
Hello, to *this* mother, to *this* boy.

After a rain, sometimes a Fairy Ring!
How they come there,
a golden circle in the grass
big enough to stand in and spin,
is a mystery she left untouched
    by the science of fathers.
I still don't know.

One gray afternoon
with the long hill home growing darker,
mittens crusted with ice, exhausted,
I begged her to stop.
    The world had finally found us.
I sat on the curb, cold, colder,
drowsy, lure of numbness.
"I can't," I pleaded.

Beyond coaxing with hot cocoa
this was one wish she would not grant,
the strength of the sun under her skirt.

And so now I say, hello.

Hello, to the sun rising, hello
to the hellos waiting to wave in each day,
to the mornings
my mother gave me, insisting
I go on.

The Sky Here

CRAZY LOVE OF THIS PLACE

I write of place as it moves me
along this stream of sun. I think
of facing up current or down
for that's the nature of it here.
The knitted skull bones of earth dive
into one another, ripple as ranges;
lichen of time crawls for light;
    trinity of water.
I am holy in this instant of knowing.

All night, trains in the yard howled
like wolves bringing down calves, visiting
prey, working up and down the valley
in the light and shadow of a gibbous moon.
In my bed I worked alongside them
bringing villages from my dreams into the world—
    or perhaps the other way around.
In the morning I dressed fully in a body,
glad to be with you once again.

In the dark before dawn I fumble
with my wedding sash and emerald crown—
my life is a book of the dead,

every day is an inner door.
   We're companions here.
When I follow this stream to its beginning
I fall as a split rain drop
east and west—fusion, fission,
oceans holding hands, my heart
beaming with yours into space.

I could just as easily die on this page,
now, or anytime in your mind, bloom
as a newborn star into your being—
this infusion of crazy, crazy love.

BACK FROM ABROAD

We talked about the wind
like we'd had dinner with the Queen,
intimate with personal affections, but nobody
had seen her in weeks and now
arrived twisting on her heels
and heaving commands we hunkered down,
the knives she threw telling
where the empty places were.

Trees lose their limbs over
this kind of love, crack right in two.
Up country they're getting
hammered with rain, the gifts
she brings riding hard with forty horsemen.
Nothing here is duty free.

You're Watching Thousands of Sunsets

With only the lights of one
distant ranch house the cold road
and wet sage meet with intermittent stars
shifting through thin cloud cover
in a seamless basket,
close enough to touch—far from here.
I don't see any eyes moving in the desert
but I hear the dark.

Gravity and breath keep me
pointed humanwise toward whatever
The Great Flowering brings to mind.
The absence of time is folly,
but the shape of time is
not a line, nor a dot, but in love
with its own reflection.

At meridian a lunar eclipse
is in progress. Why red?
Go there—put yourself on the moon
looking at Earth which is passing
in front of the Sun. Every point
on the terrestrial horizon is a sunset

throwing a crimson-orange glow
on lunar dust where you stand.

Now, come back to Earth
and watch yourself, silent and proud,
sailing your rosy ship
just off the coast
of your home planet.

WHAT WATER BELIEVES

This water has nothing to believe;
the Maker of Days already believed it,
believed it clear as the word,

full of light, anybody's story;
believe it to be the sun looking back
on itself, the cooling rock.

This water needs nothing to grab at;
each stem of red grass is already
that channel receiving

sleeping deer, the dancer's foot,
the song of everything
glad for gladness.

What travels here knows water
as scout, librarian, lover.
The bowl above us, upside down

on the hearth, catches every tear
sent to heaven. There's more
sky underground; infinite ways

to meet at the river, burst
the egg-shaped dream.
This water hopes everything.

Let Go the Mountain Slowly

The long drive down canyon
drops past dead cafés, songless burials,
the cavernous hush of hibernation.
Who walks the edge of this road at sunset?
    What disappears here

into the shifting earth are bones,
car fenders, half burnt letters—
each one a true love story. Tragic
or completed, there is no other.

There are too many of us here to blame
and too little light left
behind Black Mesa. The sun
was red and big and it trembled
on its way down—now smoke
cools, sinks, settles in the lowlands.

Attempting to climb the foothills
empty crosses cross themselves
    for no one. Prophets
spray paint bridges and write behind bars.
Where are the tears that would redeem

this halter of highway riding the river,
the blue streams that glow
from crooked windows?
   Has she forgotten how to cry
for her children in the ditches?
Dry is the layered canyon

fading pale purple to black;
dry are the old songs
whistling on the surface of the water;
   dry is the corn in the rattle.

Dogs thread unnoticed through tall weeds.

Sharp and shallow is the night
in headlights. I promise,
I'll keep only your stories alive.

What I'm Talking About
for Maggie down river

Duality, that's what she was talking about:
zeros and ones, yeses and noes, the code
of the home universe.

Inside, the house was filled with talkers,
candles, posole and carne adovada,
sweets everywhere—
a retirement party on the first day
of the new year: solstice
for those of us who keep our days
by measuring our nights.

Outside, dark trees touched overhead
in cloudage backlit by the moon tugging
this desert city back to the sea.
She was Fire Keeper, tending
the mouth of a terracotta chiminea,
holding the light, sitting for others,
handling clear-heart cedar.

Within, the transcended eyes
of tree souls glowed as coals, red, white.

Flames, turned inside out and otherwise,
took turns, rough then tender. For a while
I handled the sticks. She and I.

Without, the moon had plenty of pull—
Him or Her, depending on your culture (in India
the moon and rabbit used to be male,
fierce in whiteness, hypnotically round).
In the end —or the beginning as it were—
we tossed each other, naked, into the fire.

Duality, that's what I'm talking about.

STREET ART

"Tag on the rich and paint for the poor."
Albert Rosales

Not all on the walls
of Alburquerque is iconography,
but something vital here
has been born from corn,
    birthed in the trembling
of east/west trains,
come down from the mountain.

How many Virgins
    it might take
to save the world depends
on roses blooming at her feet
at 10th and Lead, a good corner
for a haircut and the kind of miracle
that leaves you standing.

A star explodes in heaven, then
rises from the desert.
The moon flies into the sky;
frogs dance where water will be
    and legends get repainted

in the likeness of their creators.
God, bless aerosol.

Aztlán is a migration coming
     home to itself,
one of many stories scaling
downtown canyons and
the skate-through-theatres
of North East ditches.
Sheep is also life.

In the Tower, Frederico
rides his hydraulic cloud, paints
the world upside down,
places a soldier next to peace,
amor side by side with *educacion*.
The titles on his bookshelf
give impetus to brush strokes:
   The Ancient Maya, Man's Conquest of Space,
   The Vegetable Book, Art of the Celts, Shop Mathematics.
You must bend history
to meet itself in the sacred,
see this thirsty world concave
through the lens of a drop of water.

Some buildings are unfinished
     without a rainbow.

Sometime after Noon

In this three curve town
the dead are still truckin'
where found glass mobiles
form spiral stairways to higher heavens
and today's coffee is "Good Coffee."
It says so on a sign

under a water damaged eave that looks
up and down the highway
to no one's return.
Even the stub-beaked birds
hopping the rail leave me alone
in this wedge of sunlight I found
beside a lilac, the only green
not wilted against the last standing
leaves of mountain October.
    I think maybe
half the day is gone.

Clothes on a line, mostly reds,
sway and sudden flap
between wooden poles that run
between wooden sheds laid out

upright against the roundness
of this remote mining town.
Rusted stove pipes talk

with soot in their craw,
stand crooked but tall
in a wide embrace of blue.
Stray cats, that aren't lost at all,
trot off making rounds
    while other travellers,
we mockingly call tourists,
slow down, but not enough,
on the second curve.

Flood

Riverbeds and arroyos have overflowed.
   Cottonwoods.

They've risen yellow and orange
to mesa's ledge. More
than a river's song,
they seek recesses and canyons
miles into quivering hills.
   A flood.

A flow of gold soaks into the earth,
carries away the accumulated
ideas of spring that acted out
the spiral of summer.
   It moves.

It's hands of yellow feel their way
through green, spreading like breath,
turning the Bosque into untainted sun.
Sometimes a great tide
rolls through the valley in a frost.
   Brilliance.

In the morning: a spill of honey
catching a strike of fire.
In the evening: sublime luminosity.
Who would refuse to be carried
to the sea in such a manner?
 Autumn.

River in the Middle

The ting of Cottonwood and Sycamore
fills the valley sweet side to side,
clacking of river stones underfoot.
This is your day to be simple,
and clever people can't take it from you, unless
you engage editors or turn on television. Sometimes

it snows here and the quiet amplifies
a twig or dog in the distance.
      There's time to inquire.
Other days, over on the coast,
each green life crawling and hanging
and dripping with water
twines toward the sun or stands
and breathes close by, waving
its arms when moved to—the river
settling stray thoughts.

After while people notice you
sitting in a chair; they don't exactly
smell the leaves and taste the mist
but they walk more slowly
      in your presence. The river
has that effect on people.

COZINESS

The morning sun, up,
and already low,
has other mouths to feed
further south.

We've stored its honey
in stacks of wood,
cans of fruit,
leaves of books.

Come, sit close.
I have stories
and strong hands
with plenty of heat.

Mañana Pacífica

A Mexican chair in morning light,
songs from her Celtic fiddle,
a pot of mums growing
close in a crown, pale yellow
    with petticoat of burnt sienna.
"How can I keep from singing?," she sings—

    but that's no question.
And there's no asking her this morning,
light falling easy into the room
feeling its way across the floor,
    the day already in motion,
breathing, weeping, praising.

The shadow of a wheel on the balcony
and wavelets that you imagine
as leaves play in a rectangle
of light on the wall.
    Birds come. Stir of wind.
Her fiddle, sad at times, prays
in a house faithful enough
to hold it, a thread of love always
unraveling, running the length of her.

It's not me, she says, but you in me.

Today she's at music camp surrounded
by friends, Missouri maybe,
tomorrow, again, on the road.
    It is enough to know this.
But holding the world is too much
and letting oneself be held by it,
even harder.

Her distance is not absence;
this is the way the house holds her.
The Mexican chair hums softly
against the wall; an arm
of light slides down its back.
The morning sun climbs for us both.

Rejuvenation

The sky beginning at turquoise
graduates to sapphire, keeps going.
Wisps and smears of orange and pink.

I can't gulp enough.
The cool air at sunset flows down
over *Piedra Lisa*, offers itself.

The air I am in goes on
to a pale jagged of land; the sun
takes it even further.

I am not the body drinking,
but thirst, something deeper.
A small bird wings low,

vanishes into a spray
of yellow grass and yucca—
everything the bird needed to say.

A strand of light grows east to west,
the grid bleeds through, sparkle of hive.
Contrails shift overhead.

I go down into the city wondering
if you're still here, unafraid,
once again, to want the world.

Water, These Hills

I feel water in the hills. The shape
of smooth white granite
    tells me where it used to be,
what time it is, what time is for.

I walk here, zigzagging
a dry streambed where sand
    gives way and solid stone says,
Ride the heaving with me.

There is an echo in my heart.
I call to no one
    and the call is returned.
A woman in Kansas

tucks an instrument under her chin.
I turn the canyon to catch
    its timbre and cadence.
Arriving at the mouth

of the mountain I stand
where her song has travelled.
    Lizards bebop in the sun;
distant thunder declares.

THE SKY HERE

The enormous sky here covers everything.
We live under it
    like it was made for us.
Pleated foothills flow down
to rivers that same way,
sheltered in its bow.
All creatures walk beneath it.

Blue is the widest view there is,
and out here
no one hides from it.

Knowing that your coming
means someone else's going
is a sliver of obsidian
drifting in your veins,
    sweeping close to ideas
about how the world works.

How we continuously fit
into one another
    is a dance ground so big
it takes the sky to circle it.

STILL GOING

The message is that we built it,
that array of devices on the desert
sending oscillating code:
a leader's speech, The Beatles,
DNA drawn with circles and arrows,

binary arrangements of no and yes. We think
the content should describe us, after all,
that's the way we play it here,
the next form we take is who we think we are.
It's sort of a playhouse: some sheets of tin

the bigger boys brought, card board walls,
a three-legged chair with bricks,
a window for looking out
and all the meaning we bring to that.
Maybe we'll grow up in this playhouse.

Maybe, if we have some, our parents
will call us in for dinner. Maybe
our package of radio waves
will travel unopened, forever beeping
its little earth heart into the still unknown.

SELF EMPLOYED

For a long time I was on my way
to get a real job. But the sun
kept coming up in different places
and each evening it left
whistling a new song.
I felt compelled to record all this
so I followed the shifting light,
the way it ran looping colored circles
around the world, then disappeared
behind tides of prairie and dark mountains.

Oh, it's just the sun, they said,
let's go make some hay.

One day I followed the sun
into the night, and found all
its companions in a great migration
as far as I could see;
and someone was standing
there, awestruck, looking,
but I could no longer say his name,
and there was no longer
any job but this
to which I could return.

West of Anywhere

MIGRATION

The swaths they cut
across the rolling wheat of Eastern Oregon
shook the earth twenty horses wide.
They'd have made the coast
but turning back again and again
is the bailing of America,
truck loads of bread those ponies
never knew. I kept going.
Four score later it was blacktop
all the way to Tillamook,
25 cents a loaf.

The rocky coast was as far
as I could walk—seeing further
is something I do.
Forty soft brown eyes pulling
under the sweating sun
helped make me strong.

I'm flicking my ears and whinnying
for all of us. This craggy shore
is just the beginning.

TROPHIES

In Thermopolis, Wyoming there's a restaurant
with a bar: high ceilings, stairs
winding up to lookouts, grand fireplaces,
chattering and tinkling. The menu
is pan-seared or char-broiled and not
one wall space without the mounted head

or leaping body of an animal
stopped by bullets—a Noah's Arc
from The Yukon to Borneo, Zambia
to New Zealand, a ship that never left port.
I ordered a rib-eye (beef), a dish

from the central plains of North America
grown in captivity, pink in the middle.
Twenty feet high and room to room
game rallied, protecting the calves.
Buffalo, Addax, Rhino, Cheetah, Gazelle,
faces with markings around the eyes,
strong necks taut, holding up racks,
bucks and does separated
from families. At first they just watched.

I couldn't make out what they were saying
above the din of diners as I slipped
foil out from under my potato,
their glassy eyes becoming nervous, wandering.
Then, a stampede, I imagined,
something rumbling across the continents,
but when the waiter brought my bill
as far as I could see: carcasses.

Handkerchief Mesa

He shot a man and ran.
They were of different colors: smooth
blonde of the Sycamore, rusty
brown of the *Pinabete*.
        He shot the man and ran but we don't know why
or which way or what color, and this
is one way the world forgives,
this absence of facts, this kind of forgetting.

He ran to a place named for his troubles
then disappeared—Handkerchief Mesa.
There, he told his sweetheart, I will tie my bandana
to a tree, the side upon which it waves
will tell the direction I fled. Follow me
when it's safe.

Imagine what she packed in haste,
placed in his saddle bag, told his mouth with hers,
whispered so strong into the horse's ear.
Imagine the sun getting low,
dust and hooves of the posse,
ravens who mate for life.
        No campfire tonight,

just a salt-stained rag, a ribbon of hope flying
beneath the silent flow of heaven.

Then mischief and chance had their way
in the frontier lives of lawmen and lovers,
a pesky raven tugged the knot loose,
the handkerchief now mute,
    her man untraceable.
The moon and the sun fell separately
below the hill, a kind of wrenching.

Mesas heave into mountains, mountains
gaze across the deserts they become
and rattle snakes hunt at twilight,
sometimes in vain. Darkness
can be a cold and lonely examination,
but longing is like a moon
with a face always toward the sun.

Three days in a direction (we won't name)
he took the final strip of torn dress
from his saddle bag, looped it
through a button hole over his heart,
    waited faithfully
in the shade of red boulders
for his beautiful, and cunning, raven.

What He Said with the Wave of His Hand

Holler, shout, boot 'em in the ass.
Punch 'em through the shoot
toward a future of price on the hoof.
    Cut 'em, tag 'em,
burn the family brand
into the their flanks as a flag
across summer's meadow.

Chewing tobacco helps
with the stench of cauterized flesh, but
there's no meanness here,
    just the drive-through orders
of a nation calling out for something red.

Getting kicked in the leg is your own damn fault.

Sweat and dust mix on faces,
run down temples and necks
(the only tears allowed)
while mamas
bawl in the field to be reunited.

Twice his sons' ages, he takes count

with ballpoint pen on upturned palm,
waves frightened calves through
    with a low whisper,
gentle hand over trembling backs.

I throw a boot up on the rail,
rip off my straw and let the wind
stroke my hot head and wet hair,
look over at the old man
    sharpening his blade
like a midwife,
looking easy back at me.

"Don't work 'em so hard."
    At least,
that's what I thought I heard him say.

Miners

The town of Creede, Colorado
runs up and down: sharp-walled canyons,
smoke of unwanted fires,
price of fuel and credit at the bar.

The miners went up and came down.
    They followed the ring of ore
that laced the San Juans, calling them
like a wayward angel who never intended
to take them home, only deeper
into the dead end of what resisted
the surface of earth where we do our living.

They went up in the morning. They went up
in summer, went up ahead of themselves,
hardy and determined, but only half arrived.
    How they came down gets divided
between *well to do* and *unlucky in life*,
choices that leverage the character
of this country, a standard
that measures freedom by the ounce.

I took pictures at the old cemetery,

pioneer graves up on the west side,
weathered pickets marking plots,
stones, planks and bones all going down.
    I took them in black and white
on an afternoon when the sun
couldn't holler loud enough
to be heard through the oncoming storm,
junipers twisting through unkempt tombs.

Claim jumpers and bankers
are all pretty much the same. These days
if you believe what you see
you'll mistake gold for a drop
of vital sun, silver for the meaning
of a mother's touch.

When Creede got through pushing
against the mountain it flowed out
onto the flats. Real Estate. Water.
Barons and baronesses mine derivatives,
produce themselves in full color,
but I've seen their futures
in black and white.

Out of Towners Tag Reality

The intellectuals came to town
and I touched them, right there,
on the street where their coming
plowed the stillness of our backwater,
a wake just now lapping.

The satchel he brought to the podium
pulsed at his feet, a cranium dog
on a leash, nine pounds
of power lighting up libraries
with ladders on wheels, places
I wouldn't know where to start.

Every word was a kite that could fly by itself,
    or so I imagined.
He repeated words like evil.

At the show everything that wasn't
the performers was painted flat back.
I had to wash my hands to find them.
Where he took that grand piano
is a city I'd never heard of, a hotel room
where they sent the help home early

'cause what that jazzman did
left blood on the walls and the voyeurs.
All the while he just hummed, grabbing
at keys and tearing off petals;
the lightning and the thunder finally
moving on, a buzz crawling for days

over cars and cafés, and on the water.
Someday, I thought,
    I'm going to ride
in the backseat of a taxi cab.

Alone in the Field

How farmers lose their arms
is a story tractors know
where a chore done
a thousand times turns
into a Power-Take-Off
yanking bone, winding muscle,
re-spooling the reel of the heartland,
    just doing the next right thing.

Plow shears, faulty hydraulics,
a hay truck that won't stay idled—
    the two of them alone,
man and machine in the field,
trying to anticipate one another.

At the café, prosthetics wait their turn.
Half acknowledged and lesser than,
they catch sideways glances
from rural folk hunched over
stools, trying, but not too hard,
    not to stare.

There's a lot of good hands

and fingers in those fields.

Two booths down another amputee
knocks over a water glass.
A stainless steel pincer
reaches to save face,
    redeem machinery,
get the job done right.

State of The West, 1966

After a half day of seamless mirage
the distance lost its voice
    where answering a dry stream
of overheating cars
could have missed the mark and ended up
in any number of nowheres.

That old-timer insisted we go on,
leave him as we found him living
out of his giant round car
made just after the big war.
He gave us a lift
    like we were all good soldiers.
The back seat was tore out, blankets thrown
over stacks of scruffy years that learned
to shave in the side mirror
and heat beans at rest stops—
    keeping the road west clean
from franchised freedom.

Jackrabbits and rattlesnakes had long since
learned to wait for the shimmering sky
    to turn away

from the sun right now somewhere
over the coast, the only surf rolling
across the Sonoran desert that was drifting
up against anything stubborn enough to try and stay.

Squinting through buzzing sky he assured us
    he'd be okay, pointing
to a sagging strand of barbed wire
peeping over the crest of a hill,
    saying something to him in that code
only cowboys and working folk know.

It's downhill from Barstow,
then back up again, the Promised Land
already fenced off and tongue tied
    from holding back a human ocean
it never expected.

THEN I FOLLOWED IT SOUTH

The mud held the stones tight
as it passed through that town, the river
having nothing to say that day.
    A pair of ducks looked for water,
silt and dark leaves sank
in silent eddies as I scouted
for signs of belonging;
nothing had my name.

Beyond the bridge
an empty potato warehouse,
a sawmill rotting in dust,
    the gray road north.
A winter sky stopped short,
swallowing every sound
that tried to say I'm here. I stood there
most of the day; no one came.

I knew where some people were
in some houses. The river had left
a water mark around their walls,
    made things grow, but
that was a long time ago.

So I put my hands in my pockets
and waited on the dry, frozen stones
for as long as I could.

WEST OF ANYWHERE

Where the river snakes down
through an ancient lake bed
I slapped the last of my folding money
on a bar with silver dollars
glued to the surface, past patrons
holding their blowing bones
against westerlies trying to scatter history
before congressmen back east
    could sign their names to it.

Empty pockets are a good place
to drive frozen hands
in between flagging down trucks
and cupping matches.

At Boise a black bear came
crashing out of the mountain.
Her leaving had no place to move,
the rifles behind her saying, Go west,
a place she could have thought
    she already lived. Maybe
we'll end up in Yellowstone together
hanging out in the day room

with bison, standing around,
hands in pockets,
already west of anywhere.

Overnight in Glenwood Springs

From a hilltop north of town
the train station and hot springs

were the center of a flower
around the lip of which we hiked

through coming and going clouds.
The night before, my bus ticket

ran out in the arms
of the lieutenant governor's daughter.

To her, swaggering and liquor
made the capture more beguiling

but hung over was a trail
I stumbled on, a high altitude morning

trying to sort itself out
above natural steam and working diesel.

I don't so much mind
not remembering how it went, but

if I could call her name, I'd call
down valley like a westbound hawk

tipping my wings in thanks
for temporary shelter.

Postage Stamp

In the old days you'd call this
a "postage stamp town,"
but it wasn't built necessarily to send,
and since the rates went up
we keep adding packing tape
to keep the new economy
　　from blowing it away.
Actually, it's more of a blog.

You can post a comment
on your way through,
come back four years later
and find yourself on the first page.
Nobody gets thrown away.

Every twist and gimp
given by hard winters, exposure
and sucker punches sent down
from the Capitol gets rolled
　　into the dough, a loaf
that can rise a little flat
and walk with a lean

but nobody will refuse you their table,
and the feast is a blessing
whether served from Tupper Ware
or grandmother's china—
everyone invited.

If you do decide
to mail this town to someone
include instructions on how
    to tie yourself down
against headstrong winds,
but no need for reminders

about love. This town comes
with fold-out caring,
    some popup comedy,
a sweet traveller's fiddle
sailing on down the road.

How We Get Along

Twinkle lights across the mantel
and fat Santas from the first half
of the last century
create a familiar magic—
Sunday morning,
Christmas still two weeks out,
tree-shaped candles, Gordon Lightfoot,
pan-fried bread and oatmeal.

This is just one glow of goodness
    nestled
into this small town
famous for nothing, sailing
a self made course across the heartland
using poverty as a cloaking device.
But there's no point
in expecting the worse
    though we know
these days are numbered,

but numbers of time and dollars
is a wash tub full of dirt
rusting in the front yard, Columbines

and Shooting Stars spilling out
solstice to solstice.

Last night we lit up the community hall
with remembrances, celebrated
the life and times of an elder.
The children were quiet
when quiet was called for,
   busted loose later
as they're supposed to, rocking
on the upright piano.

Food and music drew hands
and hearts together, glad,
not just to be alive,
   but for small things
done and said in small ways,
making the world
safe and handsome and rosy,
staying under the wire of promotion
by being simple
   and practicing
the lost art of kindness.

Saguache County

The thing about a high alpine valley
is the music the mountains make,
bells ringing peak to peak, a soft cascade
played by early morning wind, then
each summit invited by the sun.
All day this song.

It sings beside me as I clear brush, tend fire,
bring a load down to the house, fix the door.
Past dusk and still ringing
it's a tune in the back of my head
helping with supper, quieter now.

Under the comforter
through a square in the cabin wall
I watch night fly by, a chorus of cold sparks,
clouds throwing their clothes around.

A strain of sudden music ricochets across the valley—
the mountains!, unable to sleep.
They've started up in the middle of the night.
If the moon joins them
they'll play like this till dawn.

Not Just Another Saint-named Town

This is a town you come up to.
Up from the Interstate blurring,
from the recklessness of franchised America
where billboard promises play
stare down on the dazed and addicted.
This is a colonial town
at any elevation, houses of brick,
court and high tea, swindlers
in starches shirts, the usual thugs—
a hierarchy and critical balance
of Indios, Anglos and Hispanos.
This, is Santa Fe.

Up here the words of angels
whispered into the ear must be believed,
passed on with breath and bread.
Holy town, you have been branded,
but your heart cannot be cloned.
The direct infusion of *biscochitos*
cuts the wedding of the world
into diamonds. Sprinkle yourself liberally.

Come up from the Pecos, up

from the Rio Grande,
up from infamous trails of tears
and valleys of scorched death.
Up, Saints and Sinners alike!
Deliver me
into your narrow alleys of lilac and roses,
wooden doors outlasting their frames,
clear-eyed healers who treat me
with *remedios* and songs in a tongue
only known to children of the fallen star.

What is ancient here will not cure me,
but nevertheless is a spell I wear
on my ankles to keep the Devil
from stealing my shoes and walking around
    pretending to be me.
City of Faith, you've come
to rely on parking meters, but I'm sleeping
in the back of your church.

Remember when they washed out our mouths
with soap just because
    our words had corn and clicking
and the whisper of wild horses?
Arrows found us then, the king's men,
a ring of thieves, Wall Street magazines,
but endurance cares for its children

without exploitation. We are not
a theme park.

I pop the hood on *mi coche;*
flirt with whomever I please parading
in the opposite direction;
consult with the old ones; make
    a global fusion of music;
paint this city without permission—
all these things are done
above the color of skin and crown of culture.

Our water comes from knowing—
this, then, is what we mean by holy,
its new shape of faith now forming.
    Do not underestimate the blood in these mountains.
We have returned to the plaza.

Coming and Going

The location of the Sun and the Moon
tells a traveller in Santa Fe
the way the Apache came.
The way they left
    is a trail you have to climb
a lot higher to see.

In universities Europeans argue
over blame, wrestle the grade
of the highway back and forth,
but the pavement of ownership
rolled over bones regardless
    of where they kept the papers,
the red skin over those bones
also long gone.

East of the Old Pecos Trail
those perfect dome hills say,
    come on in,
but maybe it wasn't an invitation
to have just everyone's babies.
No matter; they're here,
running hard to stay ahead

of their own asphalt.

If those children look up
the Sun and the Moon
will show them the way out,
a way they can see
if they get closer to the ground.

WHAT TRAVELS WELL

Some time ago, but not too long ago,
the great length of river
that holds east/west council
shifted its course fifty miles,
one of the natural faults
    underlying this country.
In St. Louis the cracks are there,
hairline fissures beginning anywhere
the land starts to slip
toward the empty places,
the hollowness that's left
in the thrust of upward progress
pulling the plains closer for a look.

With its feet in mud
the upside down smile of the Arch
can only watch, all those locks
and dams and bridges and pipelines
like brittle stitches, barges
sounding their horns into a night
city planners forgot to dream.

In the old city on the Illinois side

migration was built into the charter.
Cohokia, you left earthen platforms
and structures of commerce,
then receded from local time.

Cities and ceremonies are grand ideas—
just not long-lasting.
If you can't carry them with you
        they're best left
on the side of the highway.

The Stream Through Town

In the village you came from
there are graves without markers,
lies that will never be undone,
trout gliding under the bridge.
Going back is only possible if you never touch down.

The town where boards creaked
beneath your feet and storms
knocked out power until noon
    has been carried off
one sunset at a time.

The ghosts they talk about now
are old familiar faces.
    Firelight found them
passing through the stories we helped make.
Like any good town, we quarreled
but didn't always make up.

From the water tank above
we watched the swamp disappear,
sink beneath forms, stem walls,
roofs higher than the next.
Those were our hands on the hammers.

Those were our quiet afternoons
on cottonwood stumps beside the river.
We were wild-eyed about everything.

You live in a town now
that could be mistaken
for the one we came from, the creaks
    replaced with concrete, level
and ringing like a register.

Trout rippling in the stream
cast an eye toward the places we played.
The sunlight that is their shimmering
doesn't know our failing.
I, too, am growing forgetful.